UNDER CHEAHA

UNDER CHEAHA

poems by

WILLIAM MILLER

SHANTI ARTS PUBLISHING
BRUNSWICK, MAINE

Books by William Miller

Poetry
The Trees Are Mended
Old Faith
Breathed on Glass
Skywalkers
Three Roads
Recovering Biker
The Crow Flew Between Us
Lee Circle

Children's
Zora Hurston and the Chinaberry Tree
Frederick Douglas the Last Day of Slavery
The Conjure Woman
The Knee-High Man
A House by the River
Richard Wright and the Library Card
The Bus Ride (with an introduction by Rosa Parks)
Night Golf
The Piano
Tituba
Rent Pary Jazz
Joe Louis My Champion

Novels
Parker's Blood

Critical
Passion and Paradox in George Herbert's "The Sacrifice"

UNDER CHEAHA

Published by Shanti Arts LLC
193 Hillside Road,
Brunswick, Maine 04011

shantiarts.com

Designed by Shanti Arts Designs

Cover image— vadosloginov_AI / 1097631516 / stock.adobe.com

Printed in the United States of America

ISBN: 978-1-962082-53-2 (softcover)

for G.D. Richards

The child is father of the man.

    —William Wordsworth, "My Heart Leaps Up"

I commend my Treasure to thee,
Wherein I yet survive; my sole request.

This said he turned and seem'd as one of those
Who o'er Verona's champaign try their speed
For the green mantle, and of them seem'd
Not one who loses but who gains the prize.

    —Dante, Canto XV, *Inferno*

Contents

Acknowledgments

The poems in this manuscript first appeared in the following publications to whose editors grateful acknowledgment is made for permission to reprint.

Arkansas Review: "Runners"

Aura: "Ancestor Killed at the Alamo"; "Civil War, 1967"; "The Day Oswald Died"; "Martyrology"; and "Satan at 14"

Bear Review: "A Trailer in the Woods"

Binghamton Review: "Elmer's Glue"

Borderless: "Full Immersion"

Courtship of Winds: "First Drink"

Crossways: "Burning Leaves"

Cumberland River Review: "My Grandfather's Grave"

Delta Poetry Review: "Well Water"

Evening Street Review: "Hand Carved Coffins"

Fine Lines: "Storm Radio" and "Dorothy and Emma"

Flint Hills Review: "Iron Skillet"; "Snow Day, 1964"; and "Wedding Photograph of My Parents"

Folk Opera: "The Day Bear Bryant Died"and "A Snake in the Road"

Full Bleed: "Halloween, 1920" and "Rural Electrification"

Grey-Hands Literary Magazine: "Colored Only"

Illuminations: "Harvest"

Libre: "A Can of Beer"

McNeese State Review: "Ancestral Bed"

Pennsylvania English: "Cold Wars" and "Sitting up With the Dead"

Pilcrow & Dagger: "My Grandmother's Watch"

Wavelength: "Black Cemetery, Birmingham, Alabama"

Boy Scout Field Trip

We walked up and around
Mt. Cheaha, a troop
in the summer rain.

I didn't complain, didn't mind,
found an arrowhead,
then two.

Every step we took
was one step away from
my house, the den where

my mother quoted scripture
in a loud, angry voice;
my dad drank vodka

mixed with nothing.
Down there, in the valley,
my family once lived,

Creeks who planted corn,
fished for mudcat.
My great-grandmother was one....

Drenched, we stopped
at the mouth of a cave
tall enough for even

the scoutmaster to walk into.
He held up a lantern
and pointed at the twisted

shapes. Some grew up,
others down from
the dark ceiling.

"This cave is old," he said.
"These formations
  are older than Jesus."

And we slept that night
in sleeping bags,
in a place blacker

than midnight,
though I felt completely safe,
hidden in the earth.

Ancestor Killed at the Alamo

He was a cousin, blood kin,
who hated farming
in the lower settlement,
land even the Creeks didn't want.

He believed there was gold
in distant hills, the oldest
dream of the first immigrants
whoever left home.

He didn't know there was
a fort in San Antonio,
a Jesuit mission where
other drifters, fortune seekers,

would find a common grave,
bad luck but lasting fame.
He woke before sunrise,
ate side meat, a cold biscuit,

slung a pack across his back.
It was a good morning
to leave home, hot, hazy,
fields to be ploughed

even when the sun set.
There was no road, just
a foot trail to the high ground,
the land beyond despair,

slow, summer death.
Our people found a board
nailed to the front door:
"Gone to Texas!"

Dogtrot

My people lived
in a two-room house,
an open hallway
down the middle.

And other blood kin
had lived there too,
so far back no one knew
who built it.

When I was a kid,
my grandfather
and cousins
still worked in the fields.

They ate their big meal
at noon, dinner,
then slept on
the planks as cool air

blew over them.
But cold summers killed
the cash crops,
sent them in different

directions—the rail yard
and the steel mill.
A few stayed behind,
not able to let go.

They made whiskey
from wild corn mash,
their still was hidden
in the tall pines,

known only by men
blinded in one eye by
a fence staple, men with
missing fingers.

They drank not only
to forget summer locusts,
but sweat that grew food
to eat, land to own.

The Day Oswald Died

My aunt listened to the radio
inside her country store.
I rode my bike in slow circles
around the gravel parking lot.

Two days before, I'd been sent
home on the bus—we'd all been
sent home, quiet, afraid.
Something was terribly wrong.

All afternoon, we watched TV,
the same black car, people running,
crying, even grown men
who'd never cried in public before.

Now the whole country was at church,
even my parents who never went,
not even at Easter. My aunt
ran out, ran past me down

the dirt road, towards the cotton mill.
And she was screaming, "They shot him—
they shot the man who shot
the president!"

And I was alone, thinking the sky
was about to crack open,
fall in sharp pieces. But I rode
my bike in fast and faster circles,

believing I was safe as long as I
pedaled hard. The world didn't
end that November day, though it
ended twice.

My Grandmother's Watch

On winter days, my mother took
a shoebox from under the wooden slats,
looked at pictures of a woman
who died when she was two.

There was a lock of hair
cut from the coffin, given to
a little girl who cried to go home.
The hands of a wrist watch

were frozen from the sudden snow
that soaked her hair, dress
and boots. Her face and neck
burned with a high fever.

My mother was afraid of that watch,
trembled when she held it,
twisted then twisted again
the tiny gold stem.

What if she came back, claimed
the hair, claimed the watch,
claimed her? They'd go walking
in the rain that turned

into snow, heavy steps into
that silent room where there
was no coal fire, no box shut tightly,
hidden safely under the bed.

Black Creek

A deep-water port—
the rebels used it
to run whiskey, powder,
guns.

I found it at the end
of a dirt road,
a turnoff from strip malls,
a loud freeway.

Time almost covered
the dark water over
with palmetto leaves,
a cypress branch

that rose from the swirl.
I was on the run
from a bad father,
worse mother,

no love. But I had
rebel blood—infantry,
cavalry, boys who fought
with sticks on the playground.

Some wars never end,
family squabbles,
serpent ties, the war
for total freedom.

Up the creek was an old
black man, fishing
with a cane pole—
I waved at him.

Halloween, 1920

My great-grandmother, part Indian,
daughter of a slave owner
the Devil took on the third try,
set an extra place at the table.

Before masks, treats, plastic pumpkins,
she said that night was special:
the dead walked freely—her people
told her that, their people

before them. Her grown children
made fun of her, scoffed
at a "half-breed crazy". No one
believed in things like that anymore.

She put cornbread, greens, fat back
on a tin plate, pulled back
the handmade wooden chair.
And she waited for her mother,

a child she lost to a twisted cord,
even her wicked father who always
left muddy boot prints on the floor,
to sit down, eat, come home.

Crutches

At first a fever, 103, then hot needles
in my ankle, sharper, deeper, by the hour,
the minute. My mom had a date that day—
her face tuned purple, almost black
with rage—nothing ever got between her
and a few drinks, the chance to dazzle,
charm another man.

But we finally had to go in our Corvair
without a heater, first to a drugstore
for a pair of crutches so I could hobble
through the parking lot to the door
of the emergency room. At the foot
of the bed, the bald doctor said
if the swelling didn't stop

within an hour, I'd lose my leg
from the waist down. One less shoe,
one less sock, for the rest of my life.
"What if you don't cut it off?" I asked.
"You'll die," he said without blinking.
My mother stood beside him, seemed
more glad than sorrowful—no child,

no son forever. But I didn't die or lose
my leg. An IV drip, bone shots three times
a day stopped the heartbeat of her
ugliest dream. For a year, I hobbled from
class to class until the left one broke
and sent me flying down the hall.
The kids laughed and laughed.

There were other kinds back then,
aluminum that never broke
or embarrassed. But my mother
was cheap except with herself, makeup,
plastic surgery—a pioneer of vanity.
For years I used her as a crutch, limped
on bad memories into a dark room

filled with pot smoke, prescription pills,
bottles of Jim Beam. . . . I heard she died
yesterday. Who won't forgive his mother?
What ungrateful child? One day, I will find her
grave, stumble across a red clay field and leave
my crutches there. Another step will deepen
the ground, leave a new footprint behind.

Ancestral Bed

In the country, there were few
and no one slept alone. A straw
or chicken-feather mattress was for lean,
tired men home from the field,
the time between "caint see" and "caint see,"
for women with hands burned by lye soap,
feet blistered by bad, ill-fitting shoes.
Babies were born there, too.

My grandmother came out screaming,
red-faced, eyes shut, fists balled.
She lived that way for ninety years,
survived three husbands, two kids,
one a girl who lingered for a day.
She worked jobs that would kill
most able men, drove a tractor then
a forklift at Tennessee Coal and Iron.

"Rosie the Riveter" gone bad, she was
fired for fighting on the job, liquor
on her breath. All night on the state line,
she wore a .38 on her hip while she rang
a cash register at the Jr. Food Mart.
She fired that pistol three times when
she got home to scare off thieves and ghosts,
slammed the trailer door behind her.

The iron bed frame was all that was left
of her people, the homeplace, the day
she got married at 14 beneath a pecan tree.
No one took a picture—the preacher walked
quickly away. She died on a mattress
stained with whiskey, cigarette burns,
shaking her fist in the smoky air,
in cancer's worst face.

Well Water

Raised on suburban tap water, we leaned
over the sides, looked down into a steep,
stone circle. It took forever to get
the wooden cover off, lay it on the wet grass,
hoped no one saw or heard us.

Risk was everything—the chance to lower
the tin ladle on a twine cord, raise the bowl
and skim a spider or a water bug from
the dark surface. The water was colder
than the ice in the ice maker, cleaner, sweeter

than the tap flow good only to mix our Kool-Aid in,
sugar straight from the Domino's bag.
On the sagging porch, the old people hated
what we'd become, our skin never broken
by a belt or hickory switch. They hated our

parents, too, anxious for the day to end, drive
home on paved roads. But we had
our taste of well water, something below
the red clay their lives were built on,
our secret shared.

Home Burial

One by one, the three of us
were held up to see death's
familiar face and know it.

We saw him dead, the grandfather
to all of us, a hand carved coffin
on saw horses

across the sitting room.
His lined face was like a mask
the color of wood—

one finger was missing
from a boyhood accident,
cut off by a sawmill blade.

A kiss was only custom,
our lips touching his cold,
waxy forehead.

Then we knelt on a wooden plank
at the foot of the plain
pine box.

The prayers of the innocent,
we were quietly told,
went straight to heaven.

Burning Leaves

Before leaf blowers,
plastic bags, garbage trucks,
we raked them as a family.

And we burned them
in an iron drum until dark,
a weak, failing sun.

There was nothing left
but winter, ashes
that rose and fell on patches

of brown grass. We went
inside, ate cold biscuits,
greens and fat back, listened

to a small, wooden radio....
Nothing has been lost
except the four of us in a circle

around quick, orange flames—
the sweet smoke
of an autumn fire.

Country Store

Fifty cents was enough to buy two days worth
of rock candy, a bottled coke from a cooler
that was all I knew of air conditioning. Once, I put
my coins on the counter and saw a black kid
in the back window, his eyes peering above the rim.

I knew what that window meant but had never seen
a boy there before, a real boy who couldn't
step inside the front door. I saw him later
on the red dirt road sack in hand, his coke bottle
glittering in the sunlight.

I called out to him, something my parents
told me never to do, "We don't mingle with
the colored...." He didn't answer but walked
faster between the corn rows. I tried to chase him,
tell him it was "okay" that we

could be friends. But he vanished into
the thick, green leaves, never stuck his head
out to see if I was still there, willing to trade
candies. I called out though I didn't know,
would never know his name.

Civil War, 1967

We fought it on
the playground,
sticks and rocks,
got bruised and bloody.

We won "Pickett's Charge"
stormed that hill,
drove south and burned
Washington to the ground.

The new kids were
the "Yankees," kids
whose parents owned
steel mills or were

doctors in the big hospitals.
They were born in Pittsburgh,
Albany, someplace
where it snowed.

They were scared,
though we told them
cuts and bruises healed—
they "won" in the end.

Second Sleep

In the country, before the first electric light,
they slept twice. Before and after midnight,
men and women stirred, talked about
their dreams. That was the time between

a cold supper and waking before dawn,
when the mule stood unharnessed
in the barn. All morning they cleared
a winter field of rocks. That was before

the front door was taken down, a body
was washed on the cooling board, a man
wore his Sunday suit for the last time.
Those dreams signaled more than hand carved

stones, more than a deed passed down to
the trembling hands of a first-born son: a woman
flew above the trees, another saw a fish
swimming on dry land. Thunder spoke
about the future!

My Uncle and Hank Williams

He thumped steel strings,
played standup bass in local
hillbilly bands.

More than a natural, he learned
by ear, songs he heard off
the radio, late-night music

from Nashville or New Orleans.
One day, the call came,
the chance to work, the road

to glory, no more nights behind
chicken wire, beer bottles hurled
by angry drunks.

Hank waved a pistol in the air,
drank whiskey from a bottle,
popped red and yellow pills.

My uncle said no to a long-term
contract, got married, lost a son
in Vietnam. His wife went

slowly crazy. Maybe, maybe
it was better to die in the back seat
of a Cadillac, leave behind songs

played for a nickel in every dive bar
and barbecue joint from Macon to Memphis,
the white man's blues.

Harvest

On the deck, our host kept two mattresses,
one for him, the other a guest to look up
at the stars, ten thousand above the Gulf of Mexico.

My mother dragged me there, divorced, desperate,
wired on Dexedrine, dizzy from her own perfume.
Mr. Badham took pity on her, not me. I sat

behind them, slumped against a wet pylon,
breathing salt air and listening to the weird wisdom
of adults. Mr. Badham didn't believe in God,

was lucky to be born rich, just lucky, free to drink
beer and lie beneath the stars. He believed aliens
planted a few of us here, "millions of years ago,

were coming back to harvest and eat us."
Was that any crazier than a man nailed to a cross,
the promise of something "nobody ever saw

or touched?" My mother believed in Jesus but hoped
another man would save her, charmed by her
fake breasts, her dyed-blonde beehive hairdo.

She was always primping, waiting for the phone
to ring, the first date, the first greedy kiss.
And me, I wanted the aliens to land then leave

nothing behind but beer cans and gnawed bones.
I'd be the only kid left on earth, free to walk
the beach, thank the stars that saved me.

First Drink

Small for my age, skinny to my tennis shoes, I wore glasses
with lenses coke-bottle thick. My country cousins laughed
at me from the high branches, said I'd never last a week
in these woods, not this far south.

We'd driven all night—someone was sick, dying.
My dad drank from a flask he kept in his sport coat pocket.
His uncle met us at the door, the scariest man
I'd ever seen, a tall lean ghost in denim overalls.

His eyes were blood shot; he pinched my shoulder hard
when he said my name. He asked me to wait on the porch,
let the old folks be, a shadow was in the house.
He gave me five dollars, said I only needed three—

two for anything a kid wanted, comic books, candy,
hamburgers. I had to follow a dirt trail, pay a man
and bring back a plastic jug. It was winter, skeleton trees,
the body of a dead dog with flies on it, a smell I'd never

smelled before. A fat man sat in front of a gray pot-bellied
stove; a copper wire dripped drops the color of water
into a mason jar. There was a race car with the number
seven painted on the side. He laughed at me, said this

was no place for a city kid but took the money when I told
him my last name. I looked thirsty, he said, and I was,
took a sip from the jar that kicked me to the ground,
fogged my glasses. "It's not poison if you don't drink

too much!" And the world spun like a crazy top. A crow
flew overhead. "I knew your grandaddy; I know your daddy
and now I know you!" Nothing was the same after that,
a drop in the blood mixed with blood, the circle complete.

Centerfold, 1968

Before download depravity,
body parts in every combination,
she unfolded in three shiny pieces.

My neighbor's dad never
went to church, drove a Mustang,
collected every issue in a trunk

without a lock, didn't care about
schoolboy access. But for us
they were the first forbidden fruit—

those breasts, those thighs, those curves,
lured us from rules, manners,
Bible verses recited in Sunday School.

I stole one, took her home and hid
my airbrushed Eve in a copy of *Boys' Life*
buried in a Saturn V model rocket box

safe from my sister's sneaky eyes,
her tattle-tale finger wagging with joy.
A ritual smoothed those pages

when the house was mine after midnight—
a naked nymph gazed at me for an
electric minute. Even God was asleep

though he made her to tempt me
with whirlpool eyes, dyed blonde hair,
the tongue between her teeth.

World Book Encyclopedia

Out Internet, those volumes were the only source
of absolute knowledge, crammed with facts,
objective truth.

Yellow and dark green covers, pages trimmed
with gold, they filled a cabinet our parents bought
to keep us quiet, never asked what they

didn't know. Five-paragraph reports we pilfered,
counted each word for, and each word
was counted by our teachers, even the title

stretched as far as possible. One volume
was always missing—or seemed to be—
the one we need now when we can download

instantly the exact number of penguins that
migrate annually above and below the Arctic
Circle. That volume is the key we hope to find

as the days spin, blur, no longer infinite. What is
God's real name? Does reading end with the grave—
those sage books bought on the installment plan?

Full Immersion

The first in my Sunday School class to walk down,
answer the altar call by myself, I was only ten.
Only ten but growing into a gray, confused age.
My father drank vodka from a flask in the church
parking lot—my mother was a perfumed ghost
with blood-red nails, there and not there.

I didn't believe in Jesus or the grim preacher,
the pious rednecks in metal folding chairs
who ate saltine crackers and sipped warm grape juice
from shot glasses once a month. I hated hymns,
never wanted to join the faithful on a "Beautiful Shore"
or stand like a cheated fool at the foot

of the "Old Rugged Cross". But I liked the water rite,
hoped to drown and come up someone else
with wings to fly above the new red brick church
with modern stained glass. My only ticket out
was dying in a tank behind the pulpit,
chlorine in my nose, being dunked three times.

And on that day, two Sundays later, I wore a choir robe
and rubber boots, took three steps down into
blue-green lukewarm water. The preacher held my nose
and held me longer when he called down
the Holy Spirit. It didn't work, not then
or now, not death enough but something

different for a few drowned seconds, heart pumping
hard from lack of air. My robe was soaked,
my hair wet and pasted to my forehead.
The organ cranked out "Amazing Grace" as if
I was saved, and the congregation clapped
to welcome me, a child sinner come home.

Rip Tide

My uncle and I went swimming while his wife
and mother bought pots, pans, towel cloths
on the old town square. We ran between
the saw grass and sand spurs, dove into
the high breakers before a woman's voice

cut our string. The wind was hard, the water
green-black and churning with gray foam.
A wave pulled me out, the undertow stronger
than any hook in a fish's mouth. It happened
so fast and my uncle almost caught me

by the heel in time to stop a twelve-year-old's
midsummer death. And this was death—
knocked over, sucked out to the foam's
steel blade. Something told me not to fight,
just spread my arms and float, never taste

the water or look down. Then there was quiet,
a quiet and calm I never knew in my parent's
house where laughter like a razor cut my skin
a hundred times a day, a small boy mocked
for being small at an endless

cocktail party. Pulled out, thrown back,
I didn't drown in the trough between the waves.
I didn't care if I reached the broken shore,
ever swam in the ocean again. The last of it
was light, brighter than the sun.

My Grandfather's Grave

The sky was bleached stone,
the grass yellow in the ditches.
I drove two hours out of my way
to find a gate, locked or not.

He died six years before I was born,
a man I saw only once in a casket,
a picture someone took to prove
he was dead, not out there

still drinking moonshine.
He broke my grandmother's jaw,
pushed her out into the snow.
Only middle age, late middle age

questions a ghost, an old woman
hooked into a green oxygen tank,
breathing through a plastic mask.
She winced at the sound of his name....

Propped open by a brick, the gate
swung inside when touched.
My father and aunt swore he never
hit them, brought rock candy home

in a paper sack, read from a child's bible
between binges. But they were ghosts
themselves, stoned on vodka
or Valium, bottle and pill boxes

always in reach.... I walked slowly
through a maze of stones and found his
near the back fence. Half-choked
by kudzu vines, brown snakes in winter,

his name was my name, the dates
of a short life sad runes. At last,
I cleaned it, vines pulled like deep roots
in red clay: "Father, Husband, Heart of Gold."

Hand Carved Coffins

The front door was taken down, laid across
sawhorses in the dirt yard for a child,
a preacher who prayed for rain
that never fell.

Women learned early to undress, wash
the bodies, ignore the wounds
knives made, legs broken by a mule kick,
wiped the dried blood

from anyone taken by consumption,
the cough that rattled every nerve
and bone. In the shadow
of a spreading oak tree,

the men made wooden boxes,
sanded, nailed, made airtight against
the groundwater. They drew
with a final blade a cross in a firm

pine board, prayed in silence
then thanked the God who passed
them by like the shadow of a hawk....
If a man lived long enough, his coffin

was as small as a child's, his body
shrunken by wind and drought, bad luck
then worse, the time the sun kept
in the hard blue sky.

State Fair

For two weeks, the Ferris Wheel
turned above the iron shed
where the year's largest pumpkin
was weighed in a cattle scale.

There were rough edges—whiskey
on the carney's breath as he locked
riders into bucket seats, the bar
slammed down as if forever.

Out beyond the popcorn and hot dog
stands, the barker lured the bravest
into a tent of penny horrors,
the cheapest, strangest thrills.

"Dog Boy" and "Sheep Child" were
suspended in jars of embalming fluid.
Knotted, white, fist-like abortions,
they stared through the glass,

their only wish to be pitied. God's worst
mistakes were not soon forgotten,
returned in dreams that made winter real,
a hard freeze certain.

Snow Day, 1964

Gray days, ash skies forever,
trees like stick men
on the square suburban yard.

Flakes were sometimes seen,
caught on tongues, melted
or tipped the grass with white magic.

But that morning, the sky gave more,
fell apart like a flour sack,
and the whitest white we'd ever seen

closed the street to traffic.
There were no plows in our south,
sand or ice salt, none needed.

We made snow men, midgets really,
splattered each other with snow balls.
Our fathers were home, stuck,

laughing like kids themselves
in overcoats and wet slippers.
We buried them beneath handfuls

of snow, dragged them new to their feet,
unfathered. By dark, the snow
had melted, though a few clumps

remained like dying magnolia blossoms.
Our fathers went back to work
in green humpbacked cars, came home

to sit in the same corner chairs, ice
in their whiskey and on their frozen tongues,
as if it never snowed at all.

Iron Skillet

Passed on, passed down from hand
to grease-stained hand, it hung
on a nail above the coal stove.

New wife, new mother, she fried eggs,
flipped johnny cakes, until the fields
called like a church bell.

More than this, the handle grasped,
raised, was warning enough
for a drunk husband in the doorway.

Moonshine burned off fears
of one bale shy, the first green locust
in the summer corn.

But if he touched her, ripped her
cotton dress, tried to drag her
to the floor, she had a solid reply—

the blow that split his scalp, dropped
him in his bones and whiskey smell,
left another dent in the black rim.

King Charles

Black, gay, skinny, teeth missing from both rows,
he acted like a royal in a city that hated
"niggers" and "queers" like no another.
Birmingham, rednecks, steel mills, water hoses
and attack dogs, my hometown.

I worked six nights a week in a restaurant
between the railroad tracks. Charles was wiser
than the Yankee managers who hated him,
especially when he said, "I'd rather be the pain
than the ass." His father didn't live

in his head while mine owned me outright,
almost choked me to death when I said
I was leaving for Canada not jungle heat.
Charles lived in the projects. I drove him home
after work and saw the houses were

like barracks or assembly-line prison cells.
He was fired for cooling beer in the salad freezer,
his own stash bought with his own money.
Official policy was sharper than a bulldog's teeth.
I never saw him again except when I remember

how he laughed at white people, black people,
fathers who hated their children, their own sons.
He once told me, "You got to be a father to your
own self, cause when you die you're dead,
graveyard dead!"

Colored Only

What did I know except a small child's thirst
in Jim Crow Alabama? I couldn't read just pointed
then touched that fountain, almost cried when
my mother slapped my hand away. "Don't touch it!"
she said, "that's for coloreds."

Black, white, young, old, I didn't care and don't care
though I still get thirsty and hate the south
I left 40 years ago. I hate the mother who didn't
let me ask "why" just said "don't" a dozen times
a day multiplied by years. Hate was her sign

bitter as the gin she drank and never mixed
with water. All day, all night, she waited
for my father to come home from the golf course,
the card game, the women whose names
she didn't know—the man she hated most of all.

Evolution Ashtray

The young preacher put real wine
In the grape juice glasses, didn't tell
a single Baptist soul they'd drink
the blood of Christ straight from his veins.

The preacher got fired, was badly shamed,
though my mother liked his looks,
thought he was different from the men
she dated, called her late at night.

He came for lunch, sat at the kitchen table,
smoked and put his butt out in a yard sale
ashtray unlike any other. A fish, a crocodile,
an ape, a man who walked upright

brought the whole house down, knocked
the picture of the blue-eyed, blonde-haired
Jesus from the wall. "I believe that, too,"
the young preacher said and sighed,

"but where do I go now?" My mother wanted
more than faith in the god of science—
a man who would change everything,
but the preacher said goodbye,

walked out in the pale afternoon sun.
I kept that ashtray in a box beneath my bed
and thought I'd walk upright one day,
walk out into different rays of light.

Guilt

It was him, the neighbor kid—
he picked up the wounded bird,
threw it into the sky.

The bird fell down harder
the second time, thrown from
my hands, a blackbird

with wet feathers, a frightened
black eye. He fell to the sidewalk
and flapped for two boys'

sick pleasure. That was nature
in our cold suburb, our parents
cruel to us, each other.

His house was noisy, mine filled
with quiet hate like poison
from a gas stove.

It felt good to be cruel,
mock and maim something
weaker than myself

but only for a few seconds
frozen in that bird's black eye.
The sky was indifferent,

flat, gray, like the floor
of a house where nothing
really lived, laughed or loved.

The Golden Rule

Hickory smoke rose from
the stone chimney
all day into night.

We went there, my mother
and I, before the long drive
between coal hills,

the long drive to an
empty house.
The green shack on

the edge of the highway
was the last place
to eat for hours,

the last place where
people talked, laughed,
seemed happy just

to be alive. We sat down
in a booth, ate barbecue
sandwiches, drank cokes

from thick glass bottles.
And for a while we weren't
drifters, lost souls

who spent the weekends
at a cousin's house
just to be around

a noisy family.
Blacks and whites ate
side by side,

no questions asked—
the owner always said hello,
even knew our names.

Runners

In the grocery store, in the shadow of the last
working steel mill, we talked about the future,
watched the sky fill with soot and clay.
He was lucky, the kid who'd run between
molten streams, a union boy who did
whatever he was told, all his tomorrows

in a place hotter than hell. But it was life,
the only life his father and grandfather knew.
The sparks that put out an eye bought
a frame house, a yard with a pepper tree.
I ran, too, or soon would, farther south,
all the way to the riverbank where

vagrants sleep with knives in their hands.
My father tried to kill me, almost choked
me to death when I said I running north
to Canada was better than dying
face down in a rice paddy. My mother
was a harlot ghost, dizzy with speed,

from the lure of men who bought her
for a few drinks, a night on the town if she
was lucky. He ran, most likely to an early
grave, and I am running still, homeless
in the wet grass, watching a coal barge
drift slowly by, older by a day.

Wet Brain

The last time I spoke
to my father, he didn't know
the name he gave me.

A thousand miles apart,
I called him—guilt and fear
dialed the numbers.

He tried to kill my soul
when I was a kid,
forgot to pick me up

from school, left me
in a cold car to drink beer
all afternoon in a roadside tavern.

If I didn't say "sir", he slapped me
with his eyes then the back
of his hand.

But his mind and body
fell slowly apart, a quart seal broken
every day at the end,

another at midnight. There was
a peculiar design in this
final call—strangers speaking

with blind tongues while glass
shattered, his bruised corpse
sheeted, the logic of a nightmare.

Wedding Photograph of My Parents

A near perfect couple, right off the cake,
my parents' courtship was finally complete,
the picture snapped in a chapel rented
by the half hour. My dad needed a drink,
vodka with an onion, "vermouth" whispered

over the frosted glass, his favorite trick.
My mother loved her face more than she loved
her new husband, more than anything
in a world of dirt-road, red-clay poverty,
drought like a ghost in the summer cornfields.

His drink fueled big dreams of big money.
Capped teeth and a golf tan were unheard
of in his shotgun house behind the railroad cars,
a mother who drank all night though three beers
were enough to terrify her son.

She waved a .38 pistol in God's face, threatened
to put a bullet between his bully eyes....
My parents believed in the movies more than
any hillbilly preacher, muddy creek
baptism, the lingering stage kiss

while the screen credits rolled.
Little movie star people, Tony and Marilyn,
they were anxious for the liquid burn,
the mirror my mother checked so often
to see if she was still there.

Maypole, 1965

Outside the gym, between the south gate
and the garbage cans, they danced
in the hazy, afternoon heat.

Gym shorts—dowdy by today's standards—
concealed healthy brown thighs—
their breasts bounced inside

industrial strength bras. They danced
that dance , moaned, cursed softly,
not knowing why the ugly pole banners

tied like party ribbons mattered to them—
girls who would burn their bras
in a few short years, pop the magic pill

that cut the male baboon down to his
proper size. Not even the oldest
teacher really knew why they ran

the girls in a crazy circle. Her whistle
and clipboards were ugly appendages
grown over forty public school years.

The boys plainly got it, though any fool
could see it was a penis, girls forced to spin
and dance a springtime dance older than

concrete, any brick wall. Those boys were
dumb and horny, though the whistle stopped
everything but lust, changes in the heat.

Rural Electrification

A single, naked lightbulb, a single line
stretched across winter fields, brought the new century
to my grandmother's house. For a hundred years,
firelight, oil light and candlelight dimly lit
a two-room house.

How many fears, secrets were shared
in the glow of warm coals, the wick burned
almost down? Stories of men and mules,
eyes put out by a fence staple, maimed hands,
scars that made the past live—

stories of courtships beneath a spreading
oak tree, weddings on a windy day.
They waited in a circle, stood on uneven boards
between pine logs, held my mother up
to pull the twine cord, made sure the miracle

was real. The light was so bright, so painful
to look at, she almost pulled the cord twice.
but there was no way to stop a single, naked bulb,
a burning filament, no way to see anything
except how poor they were—

homemade furniture, clothes stitched
and stitched again, the dust that floated
in the too-bright air. A second bulb
would follow, a third, streetlights,
new houses built on the soil that made them.

They slept better in total darkness but didn't
whisper, laugh, tell the story of how their people
walked into the valley behind creaking wagons,
walked into the land nobody wanted
on bruised, broken feet.

Problem Child

My mother told me I was one, said her boyfriend
wanted to marry her but didn't want another child,
especially me. It was raining that night in the car,
her face silver and cold against the glass.
She really hated me.

And so I read, wrote weird stories about children
who pushed witches down wells, then filled
the wells with heavy, moss-covered stones.
They stay buried, never rose to witch again.
She stayed buried there.

God bless the problem child or curse the God
who made him, put a black tongue in his mouth,
a poison quill in his hand to write and rewrite
his crooked tales—there is some hope for him
but no future.

Wesley Chapel Cemetery

I went there to break a spell, say hello
to my grandmother's people. The Cofields
fought at Shiloh, Island 10, the British
on the edge of a South Carolina swamp.

There was no wind, no sound, except for
a distant truck on the highway to Montgomery.
My grandmother died before I was born—
her people blamed her husband,

a moonshine maker who never worked
two days in a row. A sudden snowstorm
soaked her boots, a fever followed,
an awkward deathbed scene

for someone so young.... In the back row,
I found pieces of stone, little triangles
without names or dates. These were children,
infants who died of whooping cough

or measles, the passing shadow of crib death.
They were buried without ceremony
though grief was real as a knife
twisted in their mothers' hearts.

We all belonged here, no matter the grudge,
the curse of memory. Blood is a snake
that coils in the wiregrass that grows on
the first grave, the last grave, the only grave.

Climbing Vulcan

Back then, the statue stood over
Birmingham, stood itself on top
of a stone tower—an all-morning climb
up a winding stairway that creaked
with every step. It was dangerous,

and boys climbed to test themselves,
make it to the narrow walkway with a single
iron rail. The whole valley was down below,
Vulcan above with his red torch.
Born overnight, the Magic City had

iron ore in its veins. I saw my family,
the poorest of the poor, came down
to work in the mines or build the railroad.
I saw my dad with his business cards,

many vices: golf, vodka lunches, football bets.
I wanted to jump, not to the ground but fly
towards the sun for a few minutes,
a few seconds, over all of it, them.
But I went back down,

me and the other kids, slowly, carefully,
In the near darkness, the iron spiral
swayed with every step. Bats pinged and darted
above our heads.... There was some daylight
at the bottom of the stairs.

A Can of Beer

Sober for ten years, my grandmother
"got right with the Lord," though she still
talked about her drinking days:
the all-night bars by the railroad,
soldiers home from the war.

Of course she got fired from jobs
and once was arrested for public drunkenness
on first avenue. But those things happened.
The sober life was boring, she said—
safe but boring—cooking, cleaning

with her daughter, watching the "stories,"
soap operas in the afternoon. They loved her
at the Church of Christ. A reformed sinner,
she was treated like a dancing bear,
made to "testify" at revivals.

One afternoon, alone at my aunt's house,
she said a "can of cold beer would taste
good right now." And it wasn't an idle
thought, a dark candle burned inside her,
lit by her own hand.

But the moment passed, the flame
burned out, though I offered to buy her one
she could drink from a paper sack.
I wanted to see that crazy woman
I knew as a child: loud, cursing,

prone to fall and fall again. She slept
with a .38 under her pillow. That woman
was still in there—not saved by
invisible angels—somehow still
alive.

The Day Bear Bryant Died

My father cried when the news came over the radio.
I'd never seen him cry before not even when his
own father died in a house fire. I wanted to ask
him why but already knew the answer.
All over Birmingham grown men were crying—
country club rednecks, no-neck good 'ol boys,
truck drivers, insurance salesmen like my father
who never sold a policy without a kick back
to him and the buyer.

On the green grass of Legion Field blood had
watered dreams of football glory for thirty years.
A man in a houndstooth hat smoking Chesterfields
walked the sidelines or stood beneath
the goal posts. All those men cried bitter tears
for just one more national championship.
On Saturdays, their lives of quiet or noisy
desperation were redeemed by a man many said
was born in a manger. I didn't cry but tried,
very hard, not to laugh.

Satan at 14

At the end of the sermon,
the preacher asked sinners
to stand, walk down the aisle
and be saved.

Usually, one or two did;
the organ played
and a hymn was sung.
All hands clapped.

One Sunday, not a soul answered—
not after three altar calls.
The preacher turned
red in the face.

He asked the young folks,
all of us, to be saved,
"stand up, stand up!"
And they did, walked

in a single neat file,
all of them except me.
My curse was reason:
baptized at 10, I recalled

rubber boots, a choir robe,
how I was held under
three times, almost drowned.
"Once saved, always saved!"

echoed in my head....
All eyes were on me
and it seemed God himself
held his breath.

But the walls didn't crumble,
stained glass shatter.
I sat there in silence,
proud as the evil one

with his questions,
though that wooden pew
was cold and hard as stone,
lonely as hell.

Alabama History

Our textbook told
two stories:
Creek massacres,
Andy Jackson on his horse,

rockets and space
explored, conquered.
Our teacher taught both
as if they were

the same happy tale,
progress, destiny.
But there were missing
chapters, police dogs,

and fire hoses,
the Sunday morning
a bomb blew up
the black church,

four little girls died.
The TV didn't lie
or the radio,
or the flames in the valley

where the poorest
people lived.
And some of us
had Creek blood,

though our mothers
told us not to talk
about it—only black blood
was worse.

But we all wanted
to go to the moon,
plant the American flag,
wave back to the earth.

Storm Radio

In the white, plastic bathtub,
in the center of a brick house
with stormproof windows,
my aunt crouches like a frail soldier.

The veteran of bad sky days,
black then purple, the rope cloud
twisting from heaven's killing floor—
she knew the drill.

Her girl cousins filed first
into the pit, boys next,
while her grandmother lit a lantern
that shined on earthworms

crawling in the dirt wall.
No freight train was louder, more
a freight train than the wind
that crashed through barns,

hurled a rocking chair to the top
of the tallest pine tree,
knocked gravestones over....
In the bathtub, my aunt is five

and sixty-five, thinking about the war
God waged against his people,
against her, how she was taught
to curse everything but his name.

Her husband was killed in everyday action.
She got a three-cornered flag after
her son stopped calling from Saigon,
his last letter lost in the mail.

The radio squawks—watch, warning,
almost the half second before her house
is dragged skyward, her hair pulled up
by the black roots....

The battlefield is combed
for pictures, one picture—a family
on the porch of an unshaken farmhouse,
waving from home.

Dorothy and Emma

The bluest eyes, the blackest hair,
breasts that sharply drew
the eye of every man in the field,
drifter by the fence rail,

belonged to her. Her cousin dreamed
a future, pointed to the clouds,
the shapes of wagon, cities,
a house castle strong.

The lump was small as a piece
of coal, the one shook out from a bin,
never burned. But it grew, slowly,
painfully, with roots the doctor

said only money, weeks in a hospital,
could pull out, cure. A breast cut
neatly might cost her family
their few rough acres, a farmhouse,

a bale of cotton grown to hedge
spring bets. Emma said no to the doctor
with sad eyes, the hope of marriage
to any man willing to trade

for a mule, the rows she'd hoe
in the kitchen, between the well
and iron sink. She and Dorothy
made a pact, a secret pledge to save

her beauty, cheat the family graveyard
of a woman old by thirty,
dead by fifty. Her hair and eyes
were the only answer to gnarled hands,

a face cut by sorrow as surely
as a knife. They played like girls, picked
wildflowers, were shunned as the crazy are,
drunk on moonlight or a jar of moonshine.

And when the roots grew deepest,
she drank cups of cold well water,
ruby colored by three drops
of pain elixir.

Emma died in Dorothy's arms,
ice melting in the frozen branches,
in the hard winter rows,
weak enough to enter heaven.

Black Cemetery, Birmingham, Alabama

At the end of a green lawn, neat rows
of granite headstones,
there's a chain link fence.

All day the mowers hum a pleasant tune
as if for an evening party,
ice tinkling in cocktail glasses.

Beyond the fence are cedars with crooked roots,
tipped over branches, shadows
like menacing arms.

Some graves are sunk like jawbones
without teeth. Wiregrass grows like the stubble
on a old man's cheek.

Grief is limited to posted hours,
though few appear until a tent
is raised above a modest, wooden box.

The smell of deep untended earth is real
as the smell of unwashed bodies
in houses behind the railroad tracks.

A woman mourns on a cracked stone bench;
an angel lies in broken pieces
at her feet.

The ones she knew are still her family, their faces
familiar in this twilight at noon.
Her mother's voice calls her home.

Cold Wars

At 10:15, every Monday morning,
the loud bell rang, jangled our child nerves.
all of us, boys, girls, rolled into androgynous balls
beneath our desks.

At any second, a brilliant flash of light
would erase the entire class, scorch
our teacher's shadow on the concrete,
cinder block wall.

Home was another front, neatly mowed
suburban grass, split-level houses
a safe distance from our neighbors,
a lawn jockey by the front door.

My parents were colder than the ice
in their whiskey glasses, a fine mist of malice
between them. I learned to be cold, never fight,
looked for something more in the night sky.

My Sear Roebuck telescope was fixed
on remote planets, stars, propped in a lonely corner
of the back yard. I didn't look for a silver plane,
bomber squadrons. The nearest light
was a billion miles away.

Sitting Up with the Dead

When a man had worked his last day in the field,
rocked himself to death on the front porch,
he was laid out in the parlor, a tall candle
burning at both ends of the coffin.

Someone had to stay awake through the night,
a custom older than southern dirt farms,
as old as the hills of Connacht,
the islands off the rocky, western coast.

A banshee woman walked among the dead
on the battlefield, dragged a warrior
body and soul beneath the salty waves,
the black rolling sea.

Young people, a boy and girl of courting age,
were not afraid, looked as the young always do
for the chance to be alone,
sit on the mourner's bench.

That touch, that awkward kiss, was older
than stories half remembered, badly told,
that made a baby cry, crossed a dead man's arms
in a plain wooden box.

Halloween, 1960s

We started out as goblins,
little witches, vampires
with pumpkin buckets.

Our parents let us eat
candy until we were sick,
dizzy from the sugar rush,

passed out with
chocolate-stained faces.
But one Halloween

someone baked a razor blade
in a cookie, sent a kid
to the emergency room.

The next year was worse—
a dozen of us ate something
soaked in candied apples,

tripped for two days,
saw houses, churches, schools
swirling in a funnel cloud....

By the end, our hair
was long, teeth dirty.
We wore army jackets

the vets brought back
from the war that never ended—
monsters ourselves.

Elmer's Glue

We stuck clouds to paper,
three rainbows,
the moon in daytime,
a crow that flew.

But the best part
came last:
a palm peeled off
like magic skin!

G.I. Joe Doll

There was much to hope for in the green
and brown box, the color of jungle camouflage.
Every boy had or wanted one, begged, connived
or sulked until he got his own.

His hair was blonde, razor cut, his skin white,
pure Aryan, his eyes blue as the shining sea.
In those early days, Vietnam was only the odd
mention on TV news, a third-page story

with cold facts. G.I. Joe was the son of Tunisia,
the Ardennes Forest, the outskirts of Berlin.
He couldn't be captured or killed, made
entirely of durable plastic.

Soon, we forgot about him. His trunk and rubber
knife vanished beneath footballs and worn-out
gloves. We traded him for army jackets
brought home from the war, peace signs

in the lapels. We thought we'd never be killed,
immortal protesters wearing laurel leaves
of pot smoke, death chants raised to killer
presidents. Now we are old, half alive in a world

where drones kill with impersonal precision,
"over the horizon." G.I. Joe dolls are sold
at trade shows or online. Stripped, they are
hairless, man less, eunuch soldiers without a war.

Martyrology

At the foot of the cemetery,
in a little red house,
my great-grandmother
lived alone.

She told stories
about the war,
"the War Between the States,"
how Sherman's army

butchered their last cow,
poisoned the well.
Her brothers lost
the right to vote,

own a rifle,
a piece of land for six
long years.
But she believed

in the Lord, betrayed
Himself by cowards,
faithless men.

One day, he'd raise
the dead, hang traitors
from the hanging tree,
"let the buzzards

pick their bones."
There was a picture
above the fireplace,
a fire that burned

day and night—three faces
in a wooden frame:
Brutus, Jesus, John Wilkes Booth.

Window Unit, 1962

We played in the yard
until midnight: war,
cowboys and Indians.

On the porch, our parents
talked about their parents,
and the ones

who came from across
the ocean, the mountains,
hauled what they owned

in carts drawn by
long-eared mules.
Our house was hot,

our faces shiny with sweat—
the moon our only light.
A cardboard box

changed everything,
the metal box inside it,
numbers and knobs.

Our parents claimed it
for themselves, slept
in cold comfort.

A second unit came next,
then a black and white TV.
And the house was loud

with canned laughter,
the noise of a shootout, cannons
fired at soldiers who died

between car commercials.
We didn't sweat, run,
laugh like children

in the moonlight,
the shadows of living trees.
No one talked anymore.

A Trailer in the Woods

She worked at the Jr. Food Mart
on the Mississippi state line. All night,
standing on bad feet, a .38 on her hip
banging a cash register for minimum wage.
My grandmother never complained.

Finally, she had her own place, a *Nomad*
trailer salvaged from her third marriage
parked in the deepest woods she could find,
pines thick and standing in all directions.
No more men, she vowed, no more broken jaws,

fingers turning blue after she was beaten,
locked out in the snow. A woman who lived
alone was easy prey but not her.
Nothing made her happier than three beers
drunk at the kitchen table, walking outside

before the sun came up, firing her pistol
in the raw morning air. She let them know
a woman's trailer was a castle, too,
that cordite smelled better than perfume.
She loudly told them all she was still alive.

A Snake in the Road

My great grandmother saw it first, her Creek Indian blood
warned her bad luck or worse was about to follow.
Her husband, the preacher, pulled out his pistol
to shoot the damned thing, Satan still crawling in the dirt
where God had put him. But he shot himself in the leg,
bled out before their buggy could be driven
to the nearest town. He died, talking about God
though it seemed to her he cursed his maker for letting
a man of faith like him die in such a cruel, senseless way.
All the way down those dusty generations, our bloodline,
that snake never died.

Stubborn superstition or mere chance,
the hand of God lifted like a shadow
over sand flecked with mica. My great grandmother died
screaming about the baby the doctor cut out of her
twenty years before. Always, she wished she'd died,
had rested in a hand carved coffin from all that pain.
Her favorite son died of syphilis, and I have missing
wisdom teeth from his misadventure
in a cat house behind a cotton gin.
All snakes were cursed by God

for tempting a simple woman with sly words
on a slithering tongue. Bad luck, fate, are still
to be found on a country road where a gun
is pulled out and fired too quickly.
What was done by a proud man to prove his faith
can't be undone, rolled back like a wagon wheel
in the dust we're all made from. Another child
is born, cut out, held up for judgment—
cries in the night.

WILLIAM MILLER earned degrees at Eckerd College, Hollins College, and SUNY-Binghamton. He is the author of twelve books for children, eight collections of poetry, a mystery novel, and a critical reading. His poems, short stories, and scholarly articles have appeared in many journals, including *The Penn Review, The Southern Review, Shenandoah, Prairie Schooner West Branch, The Zora Neale Hurston Forum* and *English Language Notes.* He lives and writes in the French Quarter of New Orleans.

SHANTI ARTS

NATURE ▪ ART ▪ SPIRIT

Please visit us online
to browse our entire book catalog,
including poetry collections and fiction,
books on travel, nature, healing, art,
photography, and more.

Also take a look at our highly regarded art
and literary journal, *Still Point Arts Quarterly*,
which may be downloaded for free.

www.shantiarts.com

www.ingramcontent.com/pod-product-compliance
Lightning Source LLC
Chambersburg PA
CBHW031148090426
42738CB00008B/1261